Animal Adaptations

Senses

Megan Kopp

www.av2books.com

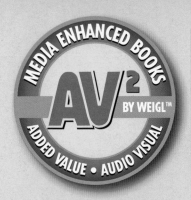

AV² provides enriched content that supplements and complements this book. Weigl's AV² books strive to create inspired learning and engage young minds in a total learning experience.

Your AV² Media Enhanced books come alive with...

Audio
Listen to sections of the book read aloud.

Key Words
Study vocabulary, and complete a matching word activity.

Video
Watch informative video clips.

Quizzes
Test your knowledge.

Embedded Weblinks
Gain additional information for research.

Slide Show
View images and captions, and prepare a presentation.

Go to **www.av2books.com**, and enter this book's unique code.

BOOK CODE

R502129

AV² by Weigl brings you media enhanced books that support active learning.

Try This!
Complete activities and hands-on experiments.

... and much, much more!

Published by AV² by Weigl
350 5th Avenue, 59th Floor
New York, NY 10118
Websites: www.av2books.com   www.weigl.com

Library of Congress Control Number: 2014941764

ISBN 978-1-4896-1382-0 (hardcover)
ISBN 978-1-4896-1383-7 (softcover)
ISBN 978-1-4896-1384-4 (single-user eBook)
ISBN 978-1-4896-1385-1 (multi-user eBook)

Printed in the United States of America in North Mankato, Minnesota
1 2 3 4 5 6 7 8 9 18 17 16 15 14

052015
WEP090514

Project Coordinator Aaron Carr
Art Director Terry Paulhus

Every reasonable effort has been made to trace ownership and to obtain permission to reprint copyright material. The publishers would be pleased to have any errors or omissions brought to their attention so that they may be corrected in subsequent printings.

Photo Credits
Weigl acknowledges Getty Images as its primary photo supplier for this title.

Contents

What Is an Adaptation?

Animals have different characteristics, or **traits**, to allow them to survive in their **habitat**. These traits develop over time, taking hundreds of millions of years in some animals. **Natural selection** of the best traits to suit a habitat happens over time. Animals that have adapted best to their habitat are able to survive for many generations, or lifespans of individual animals.

A TAIL TO IMPRESS
Peacocks are a very good example of natural selection. A few thousand years ago, not all peacocks had large, bright tails. The peacocks that did, however, were chosen as **mates**. Over time, peacocks without large, bright tails died out. Today, all peacocks have impressive tails.

There are many different kinds of adaptations. Adaptations are useful for finding food, avoiding **predators**, surviving very hot or cold temperatures, finding a mate, movement, and surviving in a changing habitat. Giraffes have adapted to their habitat by developing long necks and long legs to help them reach their food. Other animals, such as eagles and polar bears, have adapted by developing keen senses, such as eyesight and smell, to help them find their food.

5

AMAZING ADAPTATIONS

From sight, sound, and hearing to touch and taste, these animals have highly developed senses.

Cricket
Hearing

Eardrums on their front legs allow crickets to hear the calls of other crickets.

Dragonfly
Sight

Dragonflies have compound eyes made up of 30,000 individual lenses. They can see colors that people cannot see.

Komodo Dragon
Smell

These large lizards from Indonesia can smell dead animals up to 6 miles (10 kilometers) away.

Monarch Butterfly
Taste

Butterfly feet are 200 times more sensitive than human tongues to the sweet taste of sugar.

Walrus
Touch

Over 700 touchy whiskers make up the moustache that helps a walrus find food on the ocean floor.

What Are Senses?

Senses are the tools that allow an animal to gather information about its habitat. Animals need to know if there is a predator in the area to avoid being eaten. They need to be able to find food for survival. They also need to find a mate. If they do not produce offspring, the **species** will die out over time. Survival is important both as an individual and as a species. Animals gather knowledge of their habitat by using their senses.

DAYTIME HUNTERS

Dragonflies hunt by sight, chasing other insects through the air. With their flexible necks and compound eyes, they can see in almost any direction when they fly.

NIGHTTIME HUNTERS

Leopards and many other **nocturnal** animals have a special layer of tissue in their eyes. It reflects light and causes the eyeshine, or glowing eyes, that is seen in many animals at night.

Animal senses usually include sight, hearing, touch, taste, and smell. These senses build up a picture of what is or is not in an animal's space. It also shows an animal where to find food. Take away any one of these senses, and the others become more developed.

Moles live underground. They do not rely on their sense of sight as their habitat is dark. In fact, they can barely see. Their other senses have adapted and become stronger. The star-nosed mole has an incredible sense of touch. Its nose has adapted to have 22 octopus-like tentacles. These special growths are very sensitive to touch, and contain more than 25,000 tiny sensors. The star-nosed mole can feel small soil animals and swallow them in the blink of an eye.

Moles also have excellent senses of smell and hearing, but they can hear much better underground than above ground.

What Do They Do?

Some animals use their senses to avoid danger. They watch, smell, and listen for predators. If there is potential danger, the animals can use these warning signs to get away. For other animals, senses are important for finding food. In order to survive, predators must find their **prey** before they get away.

A DESERT FOOD WEB

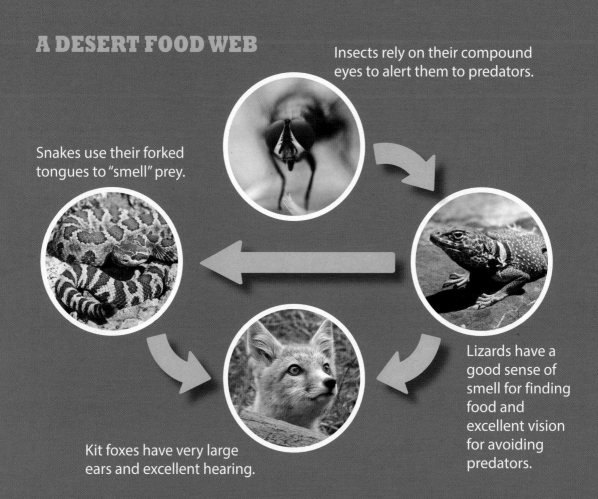

Insects rely on their compound eyes to alert them to predators.

Snakes use their forked tongues to "smell" prey.

Lizards have a good sense of smell for finding food and excellent vision for avoiding predators.

Kit foxes have very large ears and excellent hearing.

Nearly all animals, in fact 9 out of 10, have eyes. Predators, such as big cats, often have forward-facing eyes, which are good for judging depth. Plant-eaters, such as deer, usually have eyes on the sides of their heads. This allows them to see danger from all around.

An animal that has strong senses to warn of danger stays alive longer. The longer an animal lives, the better chance it has of producing offspring. Its offspring will **inherit** its adaptations. These adaptations become common features of this species.

LOOKING AROUND

Chameleons have adapted the ability to move their eyes independently of each other. This means they can look in two different directions at the same time. The eyes stick out from the chameleon's head, giving it 360 degree vision.

SEEING IN THE DARK

Owls need eyes that work well in the dark. Big eyes gather more light. Owl eyes are so big they cannot move. To move its eyes, the owl must move its entire head. Owls can turn their heads up to 270 degrees.

Types of Senses

Animals have five main senses. These are sight, hearing, taste, touch, and smell. Animals that are active during the day rely heavily on sight. Nocturnal animals usually have excellent hearing. Which sense is highlighted depends on the animal and its habitat.

Some animals have special senses. Bats, dophins, whales, and some shrews can "see" with sound. This is called **echolocation**. Some snakes "see" heat. This sense allows snakes to hunt warm-blooded animals after dark.

Sharks have a special sense that allows them to pick up on their prey's faint electric fields.

5
SUPER SENSES

Touch
Catfish have long whiskers that drag along the river bottom. When they touch food, the fish stops to eat.

Hearing
Owls rely as much, if not more, on hearing than sight for finding prey. An owl can hear 10 times better than a human.

Smell
Polar bears can smell a seal from more than ½ mile (1 km) away and 3 feet (1 meter) under the snow.

Sight
The tarsier has the largest eyes, compared to its body size, of any animal on Earth.

Taste
Rabbits have 17,000 taste buds on their tongues. Humans have only 9,000.

How Do They Work?

Animal eyes come in a variety of sizes and styles. Some animals see the world in shades of gray. Others can see colors. Birds can see **ultraviolet ligh**t that is invisible to humans. All of this information is passed along nerves, which connect the eyes to the brain. Here, the signals are processed, so that an animal can make sense of what it sees.

The giant squid has the largest eyes of any animal in the world.

Our world is not quiet. Waves of pressure carry energy. Animals feel this as vibrations or hear it as sound. Some insects have ears on their **antennae**. Some have ears on their legs. **Mammals** have a **complex** ear. Nerves send messages to the brain, and the brain interprets it as sound. Animals use smell and taste to identify food and to avoid harmful substances. Animals use touch to protect themselves, to communicate, and also to find food.

4 SPECIES USING A SPECIAL SENSE

Some animals send out sounds and listen for their echoes. By doing this, they can find prey, avoid obstacles, and **navigate** without using their eyes. This is called echolocation.

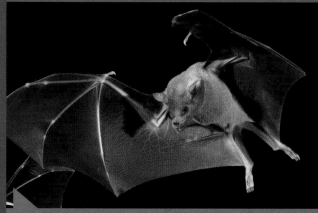

Bats use sound waves to navigate in darkness and find insects to eat.

Shrews use echolocation only to be aware of dangers in their habitat. They do not use it for finding food.

Cave swiftlets change their normal calls to a buzzing sound to help them find their way when they fly in darkness.

Dolphins use echolocation for finding prey and communicating.

Timeline

Sight is the top sense for gathering information about surroundings. From whales deep in the ocean to monkeys high in the trees and hawks soaring above the ground—sight is important for avoiding predators, finding food, and locating mates. Around 540 million years ago, there were no animals with eyes. The creatures that did exist could only sense light from dark. Animals have developed eyes over time.

The eyes of an orca may be hard to see, but orca have excellent eyesight both in and out of water. Their eyes are adapted for seeing under water.

The Development of Senses

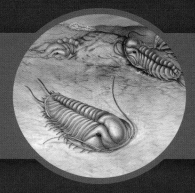

526 million Years Ago

Trilobites are the **ancestors** of today's crabs. They were the first species to develop compound eyes. Trilobites became extinct 250 million years ago.

50 million Years Ago

Crickets and katydids developed ears on their knees.

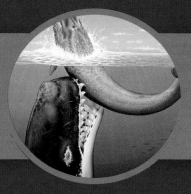

30 million Years Ago

Ancient whales were using echolocation to find food.

Today

Great white sharks have six highly refined senses. Over the past 100 million years, sharks have developed the most incredible sense of smell, hearing, touch, taste and sight. They are nothing short of amazing.

How People Have Learned from Animals

People have learned a lot from studying animals and their senses. While birdwatchers use binoculars to see small birds in trees, an eagle can spot a rabbit from 2 miles (3 km) away. This is because eagles have five times as many light-sensitive cells in their eyes as people do. Need light at night? Night vision goggles make low light brighter. This is nothing new. The eyeshine found in the eyes of animals that feed or hunt at night does the same thing.

Dogs can hear a far greater range of sounds than people can. People have developed ultrasound that uses sound waves to make images, like that of an unborn baby.

Sonar uses waves of sound that can travel through air or water. The sound waves reflect off a surface. The sonar operator listens to the echo and then calculates the distance to the object. This is the same principle bats have been using for echolocation for millions of years. Human-made voltmeters measure electrical pulses. This is the same thing sharks do when tracking prey. Long-distance vision is something **satellite imagery** has in common with buzzards. Buzzards can spot small prey over 2 ½ miles (4 km) below them.

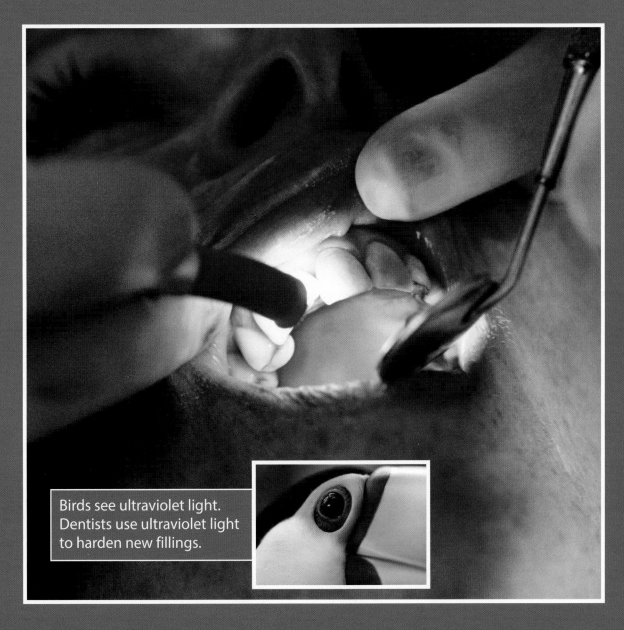

Birds see ultraviolet light. Dentists use ultraviolet light to harden new fillings.

Senses and Biodiversity

Biodiversity refers to the variety of life in a habitat. The survival of many species depends on maintaining biodiversity. A greater variety of animals in an area creates a stronger food chain. If one species were to become extinct, other animals could take their place in the food chain.

Protecting biodiversity is important for maintaining a healthy environment. People depend on the environment for air, food, and water. Biodiversity contributes to the beauty and wonder of this world we call home.

The senses of sight, hearing, touch, taste, and smell are all used to help species survive. Some species have developed special senses such as the ability to "read" an echo and tell how far something is away. Other animals can sense heat and use it to track down their prey. Still others "read" faint electrical fields to find food. These unique senses are an important part of biodiversity in the animal world.

Fire Bugs can sense the heat of forest fires from far away. They use this special sense to find newly burned wood in which to lay their eggs.

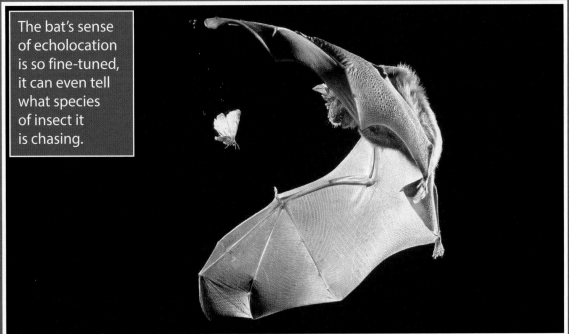

The bat's sense of echolocation is so fine-tuned, it can even tell what species of insect it is chasing.

Conservation

It is important for humans to protect the natural environment of animals that are adapted to living there. Destruction of these habitats makes specialized senses useless. These animals become vulnerable. Loss of these species harms biodiversity. Animals can be protected by organizations such as the International Union for Conservation of Nature (IUCN). The IUCN is the world's oldest and largest global environmental organization. It works to conserve biodiversity around the world.

Wildlife can also be protected by national parks.

Activity

Match each animal with the type of sense that most helps it survive.

Quiz

Complete this quiz to test your knowledge of animal senses.

1 What species of animal was the first to develop eyesight?

A. Trilobite

2 What part of their body do butterflies use to sense taste?

A. Feet

3 Birds can see what kind of light that humans cannot?

A. Ultraviolet

4 What do dolphins use for finding prey and communicating?

A. Echolocation

5 Which animal has the largest eyes in the animal world?

A. Giant squid

6 What does IUCN stand for?

A. International Union for Conservation of Nature

7 How many times better do owls hear than humans?

A. 10

8 How many years have crickets had the sense of hearing?

A. 50 million

9 Which species of bird uses echolocation to find its way in dark places?

A. Cave swiftlet

10 What animal "sees" infrared radiation, or heat?

A. Snake

Key Words

ancestors: animals that have come before in a line of development, forerunners

antennae: a pair of feelers on the head of an insect

complex: consisting of many different and connected parts

echolocation: a sensory system in animals such as bats and dolphins in which high-pitched sounds are made that then reflect off objects. Echolocation is used to calculate the direction and distance of objects.

habitat: the natural environment of a living thing

inherit: to gain genetic characteristics from a parent

mammals: warm-blooded animals that feed milk to their young and are usually covered with hair or fur

mate: a breeding partner

natural selection: a natural process where animals that have better adapted to their environment survive and pass on those adaptations to their young

navigate: to find the way

nocturnal: animals that are most active at night

predators: animals that hunt and eat other animals

prey: an animal that is hunted and eaten by another animal

satellite imagery: photos taken from space by a machine called a satellite

sonar: a human-made system for finding objects under water through the use of reflected sound. Sonar stands for sound navigation and ranging.

species: a group of plants or animals that are alike in many ways

traits: special characteristics

ultraviolet light: rays of light that cannot be seen by people

Index

Log on to www.av2books.com

AV² by Weigl brings you media enhanced books that support active learning. Go to www.av2books.com, and enter the special code found on page 2 of this book. You will gain access to enriched and enhanced content that supplements and complements this book. Content includes video, audio, weblinks, quizzes, a slide show, and activities.

AV² Online Navigation

Audio
Listen to sections of the book read aloud

Book Pages
AV² pages directly correspond to pages in the book.

Video
Watch informative video clips.

Key Words
Study vocabulary, and complete a matching word activity.

Embedded Weblinks
Gain additional information for research.

Quizzes
Test your knowledge.

Slide Show
View images and captions, and prepare a presentation.

Try This!
Complete activities and hands-on experiments.

AV² was built to bridge the gap between print and digital. We encourage you to tell us what you like and what you want to see in the future.

Sign up to be an AV² Ambassador at www.av2books.com/ambassador.